GROW YOUR OWN
MONSTERS

Nicola Davies
and
Simon Hickmott

Illustrated by Scoular Anderson

F

FRANCES LINCOLN
CHILDREN'S BOOKS

Contents

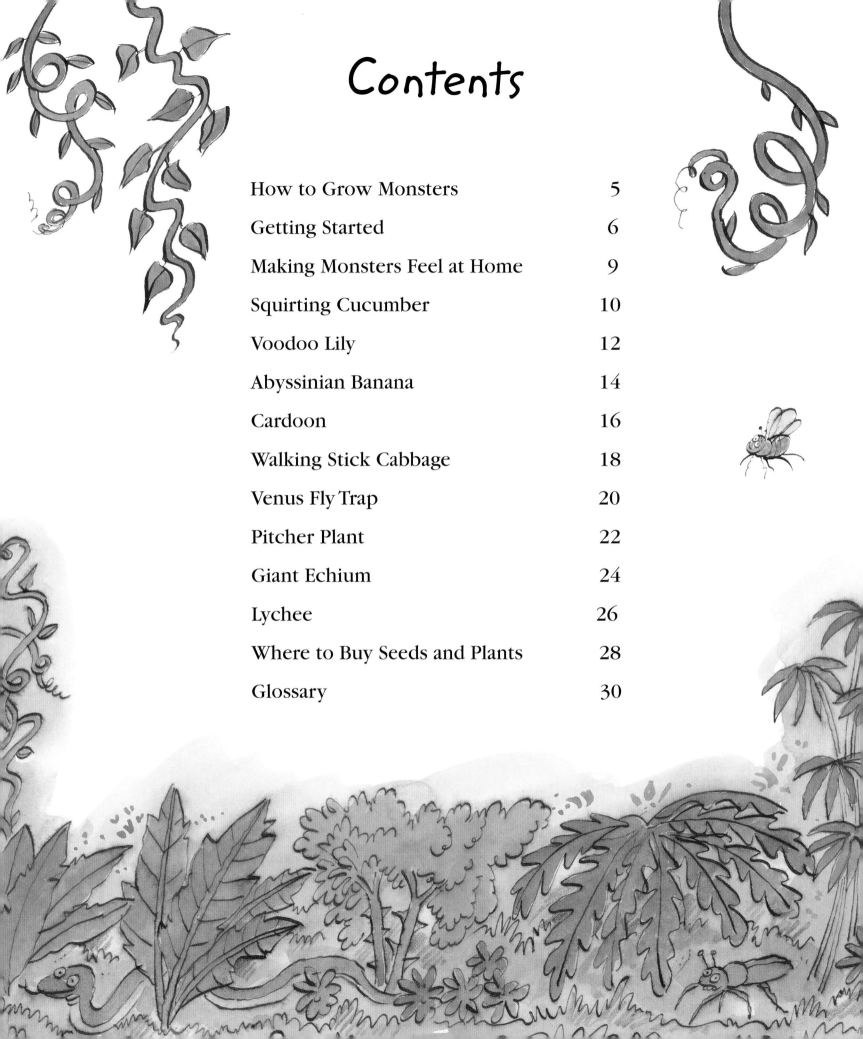

How to Grow Monsters

The plants in this book aren't pretty flowers, they are big and weird, and that's why we've called them monsters! Here are some tips to help you grow them.

We can tell you what equipment you need and we'll help you to learn some simple gardening skills for successful monster care.

The first thing you need to know is that plants want to grow. All you have to do is give them the conditions they like, and they'll do the rest.

You don't need any fancy equipment for this. Some of the things your plants will need come pretty cheap, such as light, air and water. Most of your monster growing kit can be improvised from things you can find around your home. There is very little you'll have to buy.

Monster Habitats... Good Spots For Plants

Many of the plants in this book can be grown on a windowsill indoors or need just a corner of a garden, patio or balcony. Choose a spot that gets as much daylight as possible and is safe and easy for you to get to. Don't despair if you don't have the perfect place – you can make it perfect!

Too dark? Put tinfoil or mirrors up to reflect light on to your plant.

Too windy? A mesh windbreak will slow the breeze and protect the plant – old tights stretched over a coat-hanger frame will do fine.

Monster Cages... in other words, Pots

Almost anything can be a pot. Just make sure you give it a good scrub, and make holes in the bottom for water to drain away.

SMALL POTS – individual yoghurt cartons, the bottom of tetrapax

MEDIUM POTS – big yoghurt pots

BIG POTS – old paint pots (Use a hammer and nail to make holes in the bottom)

HUGE POTS – a couple of sturdy bin liners inside a strong cardboard box – but don't forget about the drainage holes!

5

Monster Foot Covering... Compost and Soil

Most of the plants in this book need to be planted in compost. This is one thing you'll need to buy. Buy as big a bag as you have space and money for – it works out cheaper in the long run. Get general purpose compost. Go for the 'peat-free' sort – you don't want to make plants from peat bogs homeless! Some plants (like the Pitcher plants on page 22) need soil-free compost.

Watering Monsters

All plants need water, even though some may need it just once a year!

Follow the watering instructions for each monster carefully... too much water is as bad as too little. Mostly when you water plants, seeds or seedlings, aim for moist not wet – so the compost should look like freshly crumbled cake not soggy pancake mix! You won't need a posh watering can – a plastic bottle with holes punched in the lid will work perfectly.

Feeding Monsters

You can buy plant food – a liquid or a powder – at garden shops or supermarkets. All you have to do is mix it with water (the instructions on the packet will tell you how) and use it to water your plants. They'll take the food in through their roots. The instructions for each monster will tell you how often they need feeding in this way.

Getting Started

In this section we'll explain some of the words we use in the instructions for each kind of monster. We'll show you some of the basic skills you'll need for growing fine, strong monsters.

Seeds... Baby Monsters

Many of the plants in this book are grown from seeds. They come in lots of different shapes and sizes but they all need to be kept cool, dry and dark until you are ready to grow your monster.

Sowing (that's the proper word for planting a seed)

1. Sow seeds in pots and cover them with compost that is twice as deep as the seed is long.

* For tiny seeds (like the Giant Echiums on page 24) this means sprinkling the seeds on the surface and putting a little bit of compost on top.

* For big seeds (like the lychee on page 26) this means planting the seed 4 or 5 cm (1½ - 2 inches) deep in a medium-sized pot.

2. Water your seeds and put them somewhere warm – on a windowsill or in a home-made light box (see page 9). Don't let them get dry or cold, and in time the seeds will germinate (that's the proper word for when a seed begins to sprout) and begin to grow into baby plants – or seedlings.

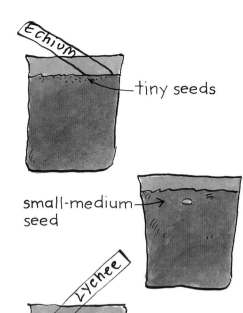

tiny seeds

small-medium seed

big seed

Pricking Out

As seedlings grow, their pot may get a bit crowded – then it's time to prick them out. This means taking the strongest seedlings and giving them their own space to grow in.

1. Gently loosen the compost round your seedlings so their roots are free.

2. Look for the biggest, strongest seedlings. Very, very gently pick each one up by its leaves.

3. Make a little hole in the compost of a new pot with your finger.

4. Put the seedling's roots in the hole, and gently press the compost around them. Don't plant it too deep, or too shallow. Just the same depth as it was growing before is best.

5. Water your pricked-out seedlings, and keep them out of bright light for a day or so. They'll probably go limp and look a bit ill, but don't worry, they will perk up.

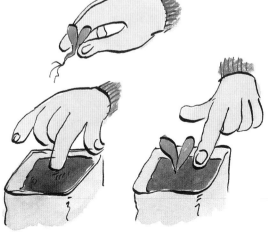

Planting out and transplanting

This is just like pricking out, only bigger! When plants outgrow their pots or are ready to be planted out in a garden you need to very gently dig them up and very carefully replant them, where there is more room.

Make sure the new hole you dig for them is not too deep or too shallow, but wide enough for their roots to spread out. Fill the hole, and press the compost down very firmly all around your monster, so it doesn't blow over in the wind. Then give the newly planted plant a good drink!

Other sorts of baby monster

Some monsters (like the Voodoo Lily on page 12) are grown from bulbs or corms. These are a lot bigger than seeds, and need different signals to make them grow... some need to be wet, some need to be dry. Read the instructions for each monster carefully to tell you what to do.

More Monsters... saving seeds

Plants are generous and make more of themselves for free. The *More Monsters* section for each plant will tell you how to make the most of this to get more plants to grow next year, or give away to friends. One really good way of collecting seeds is by putting a little bag made of old tights over the flowers when they have started to die. When the seeds are dry, store them in old envelopes somewhere cool, dry and dark.

Making Monsters Feel at Home

The monsters in this book come from different habitats all over the world, but the growing instructions for each plant will tell you what you need to do to make them feel at home where you live. Most of the plants in this book can be grown, with help, in most places, but if there's a plant that really won't grow where you live, then the instructions will tell you.

Read the growing instructions carefully and they'll help you to create just the right conditions for your monsters to thrive.

The Monster Light Box

This easy-to-make light box will help you to give seeds and seedlings the light and warmth they need, even if it's a bit chilly where you live.

Find or make a cardboard box to fit the spot where you want to put it – a nice light windowsill for instance. Cut the sides towards the light low, and keep the sides away from the light higher.

Line it with something waterproof – a dustbin liner is great. Line it again with tinfoil. The foil will reflect light and warmth and make a hot mini climate inside the box. You can make a polythene lid to keep the warmth in at night.

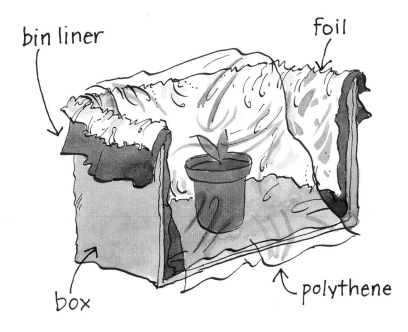

bin liner

foil

box

polythene

Mini Greenhouses

When your monsters get bigger, you could plant them in a larger pot, or put them outside on a balcony, or in the garden. If you live somewhere cool, but your monsters like heat, here's how you can keep them cosy...

Bottle greenhouse

Cut the bottom off plastic bottles or cartons to make individual greenhouses (but don't forget to water the plants inside!)

Pyramid greenhouse

Use sticks to make a pyramid frame, then stick polythene or bubble wrap when you need extra cosiness, over the top. You can make this quite big. It's a the perfect portable greenhouse for monsters that need warmth or a bit of protection on cold nights.

Squirting Cucumber

Stick 'em up — I've got a cucumber!

The squirting cucumber is a plant with secret weapons – seed guns! First, the hairy leaves and stems grow like crazy. Then the sausage-shaped fruits swell up, like overfilled balloons. At last, the cucumber fruits are so heavy with ripe seeds and water, that they snap off from their stalks and cucumber seeds shoot out – at more than 60 mph! Seeds can shoot right over walls and houses, and if they hit your skin – ouch! So watch out! Squirting cucumbers are tough and they'll grow almost anywhere. They can even survive cold frosty winters, with a mini greenhouse to keep out the rain and the worst of the cold.

What you need

Seeds (see page 28)	Small pots (see page 5)	Gritty compost (2 parts compost, 1 part fine grit from the garden centre)
	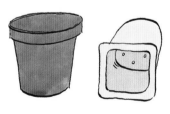	
Light box (the one you can make from instructions on page 9)	A balcony, garden or yard... any bit of space outdoors will do	A mini greenhouse (see page 9 for how to make one)

What you do

(1) Fill pots almost full with compost.

(2) Sow one seed in each pot, and then cover up (see page 7). Don't use all your seeds at once! Keep some in case you need extra – (see step 5).

(3) Put the pots with their seeds in your light box on a sunny windowsill. Squirting cucumbers are from the Mediterranean, so they like to be warm. Cover the pots with polythene if nights are cold, and remove again in the morning.

(4) Keep them watered, but not wet. The compost should feel moist, not sodden!

(5) In three weeks you'll have baby plants! If nothing comes up, try again with the seeds you've kept back.

(6) Once the little plants have 3 or 4 leaves, plant them outdoors. Anywhere will do, they don't need good soil or feeding, and unless it's very, very dry, they won't need watering either. If it's still cold at night, especially in Britain and northern US, use a home-made mini greenhouse to protect them until nights get warmer (see page 9). Then... sit back and wait.

More Squirts

Put a bag made of tights over a couple of your nearly ripe cucumbers... this way you can save the seeds and have some more to plant next year. Dry out the seeds in the sun, on kitchen paper or toilet roll, then store in a cool, dark, dry place until you're ready for more shootin'!

Troubleshooting

If you live in a city, or if you plant the cucumbers on a balcony or rooftop, insects may not get to the flowers to pollinate them. You have to be the bee! Use a brush, a tissue, or your finger to take yellow pollen from the male flowers (which look like THIS) and rub it on to the female flowers (LIKE THIS).
Remember, no pollination = no cucumbers!

fat bit behind the flower - females only

Voodoo Lily

Looks like a snake, smells like a corpse and is... a flower?

Flowering time for the Voodoo Lily is funeral time for most other plants and animals. Voodoo Lilies live in tropical countries where there is a dry season, when many other plants shrivel up and die. But this is when the Voodoo Lily blooms. Its strange tube-like 'flower', called a spathe, sticks above the bare ground looking like a reptile doing a headstand and smelling like rotting flesh.

There's a good reason for the odd timing and disgusting smell. It's flies. The Voodoo Lily needs them to pollinate its flowers. So it blooms when there are plenty around, feasting on corpses, and attracts with the scent of a meal! Smelling what they think is a nice juicy dead body, the flies crawl down into the long tubular spathe until they reach the real flowers deep inside. The lily then holds the flies prisoner with special hairs that trap them and act as cage bars.

When the flies have blundered around for a few hours and got well coated with pollen, the hairs wither and the flies are free to go. Off they flit in search of a real body, and think they've found it down the spathe of another Voodoo Lily, where once again they are imprisoned. This time, they leave pollen behind to fertilise female flowers. The spathe can last for a few weeks, until all the flowers inside are fertilised. By that time the rainy season has begun and the voodoo lily can start to look a little more normal by growing stems and green leaves like other plants. But when the dry season returns the parched leaves die and the sinister red spike pushes up to spread the smell of death over the land again.

What you need

* One Voodoo Lily corm (a small knobbly bulb-like thing. Get these from a good nursery or by post – see page 28) * A warm dry windowsill		Patience – and that's it!

What you do

Put your corm on the windowsill.
Wait until spring! That really is all you do.
The corm contains all that it needs to produce the spathe.
So don't plant it, water it or feed it at all. The corm needs to feel as dry as it does in a real dry season. You have to wait because there is a biological calendar inside the corm, and until it says spring the corm won't do anything. By early summer you should have a big stinky reptilian Voodoo Lily on your windowsill.

More Voodoos

Voodoo Lilies for next year – and for your friends and enemies. When your smelly spathe has withered, take the dry corm and plant it in nice moist compost in a little pot (something about 10 cm (4 inches) across will do). Keep it warm (outdoors if you live in Australia or the southern states of the US, indoors in northern states or Britain) and watered, moist but not wet! Now you'll see the Voodoo Lily's leaves. They'll grow all summer and into early autumn. When they die, let them wither completely, then dig up your corm. It will have grown and sprouted little mini corms. Separate the mini corms and put all of them – little and big – on to the windowsill again and forget about them until spring. The big corm will produce another lily, but the little corms are too small and young – they'll just sit there doing nothing. Don't worry. When the big lily has finished flowering, plant all the corms in pots just like last year. The little corms will make leaves and will grow, and the big corm will give you more babies. In a couple of years the little corms will start making spathes too – and you may have to move out because of the smell.

Troubleshooting

If you get to the end of summer and the corm still hasn't done its stuff, it could mean that it's just too tiny to make a lily. Plant it in moist compost. It'll sprout leaves and grow. Treat it as we just described and maybe next year it'll be big enough to flower.

Abyssinian Banana

Spectacular, exotic and on your windowsill!

This plant won't grow bananas that you can eat, but it will have huge, floppy leaves and can grow to be 3 metres (10 feet) tall. It looks as if it's come straight from a tropical island, but it's quite tough, so with a bit of care you can grow this exotic monster even if you live somewhere with cold winters.

What you need

Seeds (see page 28)

Ensete ventricosum (Abyssinian Banana)

Medium pots, large pots

Compost

A sunny spot inside or outside

What you do

① Fill some medium pots with compost.

② Sow one banana seed per pot, water well.

③ Put pots and seeds in a clear polythene bag and put somewhere really warm. Somewhere dark will do, as they don't need light to germinate – an airing cupboard is perfect.

④ Check every day to make sure compost is moist.

④ When the baby banana plants start to show above the compost, put them in the light box on a warm sunny windowsill.

⑤ Keep plants warm and moist, and give them a feed every week.

⑥ When roots start to poke out of the bottom of the pot, replant your bananas in a big pot, and put them somewhere warm and sunny inside, or outside in summer is fine. Each plant should grow to about 1 metre (3 feet) over the summer.

⑦ If you live somewhere with frosty winters (like northern Europe or north USA) bring your banana indoors when summer ends. Over winter it will lose some leaves, but as soon as the warm weather arrives it will perk up.

More Bananas

When your banana is about three years old, it will start to have little baby banana plants growing at its base. When the babies are 20cm (8 inches) tall, cut between them and the mother plant, loosen their roots and gently pull them up, and replant in their own pot.

Troubleshooting

Sometimes banana seed can take 3 months to germinate. So be patient, and if there's still no sign of a plant after 3 months, just start again.

Cardoon

Massive silvery leaves, spiny stems as thick as your arm and huge, purple thistle flowers bigger than your hand! A cardoon plant really is a monster, but it's a useful one; you can eat the stems like celery, or dry the flowers for decoration. Or you could just enjoy having a giant thistle in your back yard!

Cardoons are tough, and will put up with freezing cold and baking hot, but spring frosts will kill them. So if you live where there is frost in April, this is one monster you can't grow.

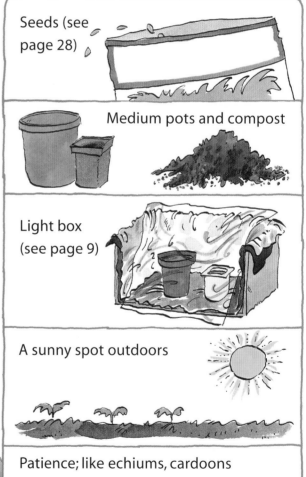

What you need

Seeds (see page 28)

Medium pots and compost

Light box (see page 9)

A sunny spot outdoors

Patience; like echiums, cardoons flower in their second year

What you do

Spring Year 1

① Sow five or six seeds in one pot (the reason for this is that the Cardoon seed doesn't germinate very well, so quite a few seeds won't grow).

② Water the seeds well and put the pots in the light box on a windowsill.

③ When the little plants have three leaves each, pull up the weakest ones and just keep the strong one in each pot.

④ When these have five leaves, plant them outdoors in a sunny spot, and give them a good water. Remember, these plants get BIG so each one needs a metre (3 feet) of space all around.

Summer, Autumn and Winter Year 1

⑤ If it's very dry in the summer, they'll need watering, but apart from that you don't need to do anything. Just wait.

Spring and Summer Year 2

⑥ Still nothing to do. Your cardoons will start to grow early in spring; all you need to do is stand back and enjoy your giant thistles appearing.

More Thistles

When the purple flowers fade, tie the foot of an old pair of tights round each flower head, to catch the feathery seeds as they dry out. Store them in a cool, dry, dark place ready to plant in spring

Troubleshooting

Cardoons can do so well in some places – such as New Zealand and Australia – that they can spread their seeds around and grow all over the place. In these places you need to pick your thistle flowers before they make fluffy seed heads.

Walking Stick Cabbage

Grow your own walking stick

The Walking Stick Cabbage starts off looking like any other sort of cabbage, leafy and green – so be careful you don't forget what it is and eat it for dinner. But late in the year, in autumn and winter it starts to get much bigger. The stem gets long and thick, and the whole plant looks so tough that you might almost be scared to cut the stem, ready to make your walking stick.

This monster likes cold winters and cool summers – it can't take the heat. So if you live where summers are very hot and dry you can't grow this plant. If gardeners in your neighbourhood can grow cabbages, sprouts or kale then you can grow a Walking Stick Cabbage.

What you need

Seeds (see page 28)

Space outside to plant them

What you do

Spring

① Make a 'drill' – this is a mini trench about as deep as the width of your thumb.

② Sow your seeds about 4-5 cm (1½-2 inches) apart, cover them up with soil and water them in.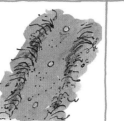

③ Mark the place where you've planted them, so you can watch for the baby cabbage plants to appear.

④ Transplant (see page 8) your cabbages when each plant has 5-6 leaves. Make sure you stamp down on the ground all round your plant's roots. This is very important. You plant will fall over as it gets big if you don't do this.

⑤ Feed (see page 6) once a week.

⑥ Let it grow until late winter, to make sure the stalk is strong enough to make a stick.

⑦ Cut off the roots and leaves, and hang your cabbage plant upside down somewhere dry and airy; a shed or a porch is good.

⑧ When it's brown and dry in three or four months, you can varnish it and use it as a stick.

More sticks

Leave one plant to grow through the winter and on into a second spring. It will make little yellow flowers and then long green seed pods. When these dry out, you can collect the seeds and be ready to grow more walking sticks.

Troubleshooting

Walking stick cabbage plants get so big that strong winds can uproot them. So firm roots (see step 4) are essential. To make your monster extra safe, drive a sturdy stake into the ground beside your monster and tie your plant to it so it can't blow about in the wind.

Venus Fly Trap

A death trap for flies

The meat-like red of a Venus Fly Trap's trap tempts a fly in with the promise of a meal. But as soon as the fly touches the tiny trigger hairs on the red surface, once, then twice, the trap is sprung: the two halves snap shut, the spines on their edges overlap to make a cage and the fly is caught. The more it struggles, the tighter the trap holds it. Soon it will be digested, then trap and prey will be absorbed back into the plant.

Like pitcher plants these gruesome killers are bog plants, that like wet feet, plenty of light and protection from winds and storms.

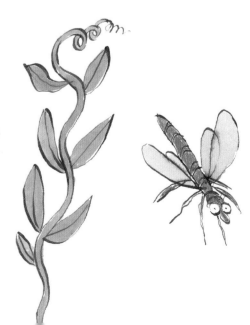

What you need

Growing Venus fly traps from seed takes a lot of time and patience as seedlings are tiny in their first year and easily overgrown by moss. So it's best to buy a young plant.

Moss peat – it's the only kind of soil they'll grow in.

Small pots – Venus fly traps like to feel cosy and don't need much peat.

The Right Sort Of Water, in other words rainwater, melted snow or de-ionised water (the sort you can buy in car spares shops, to put in car batteries)

A shallow container for water, that you can stand your pot in.

A very sunny spot.

What you do

① Venus fly traps live in bogs and marshes where there is no shade, so they need lots of light.

② It's pretty wet in bogs and marshes, so stand your plant pot in a container with a centimetre or so of water in it – always use the right kind of water. You don't need to water them if you keep this water round their feet topped up at all times.

③ VFTs need to eat flies, so in summer, put them where they can catch their own – outside in a sunny spot is best.

Ya! Missed!

④ VFTs don't like frost, but they like a cool rest in winter. Put them somewhere frost free, and out of wind and rain, but unheated and light, for the winter.

Troubleshooting

If your VFT gets watered with the wrong sort of water by mistake, don't panic. Just give it a thorough watering with the Right Sort of Water, and replace the water in the container. Snapping a trap shut takes a lot of energy from a VFT, so NEVER be tempted to set off an empty trap just for fun – it could weaken and even kill your plant.

More Traps

If you stick to the instructions above, your VFT will thrive. A healthy plant will have several open traps, with nice pinky red insides. In two years your plant will have grown and will need a new bigger pot, or could be gently split into two. Repot your VFT in the early spring as it starts to grow after the winter rest. You'll soon have a house full of killer plants.

Pitcher Plant

An insect eater on your windowsill!

We're used to the idea that animals eat plants, but surely plants can't eat animals? But that's exactly what pitcher plants do. Their vase shaped leaves are traps, where insects drown and their bodies dissolve to make food for the plant. The bogs and marshes where pitcher plants live in the wild, have such poor soils that killing and eating insects is the only way these plants can get the nutrients they need to grow.

Pitcher plants don't mind heat, as long as their feet are wet, and they don't mind cold; but they hate to be battered by wind and rain, so in winter or stormy weather they need to be safe on a windowsill.

What you need

A baby pitcher plant. (Growing pitcher plants from seed is too hard, but you can get baby pitcher plants from garden centres and plant sales. See page 28)

Soil-free compost such as perlite (see page 6)

Rainwater/melted snow or de-ionised water (the sort you can buy in car spares shops, to put in car batteries)

A shallow container for water, that you can stand your pot in

A very sunny spot

What you do

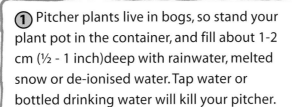

① Pitcher plants live in bogs, so stand your plant pot in the container, and fill about 1-2 cm (½ - 1 inch) deep with rainwater, melted snow or de-ionised water. Tap water or bottled drinking water will kill your pitcher.

② Pitcher plants need lots of light so stand your pitcher plant indoors on a very sunny windowsill, or outside in a sunny spot.

③ They need the chance to catch insects, so put them outside or in a window where flies are buzzing – they won't buzz for long!

EEK!

Help!

Troubleshooting

If your plant gets watered with the wrong sort of water by mistake, don't panic. Just give it a thorough watering with the right sort of water, and replace the water in the container.
Never, ever, EVER feed your pitcher plant and don't let it ever dry out.

More Pitchers

As your plant grows, it will make more and more pitchers. You can gently pull these away from the parent plant, carefully loosening their roots. Plant them in a new pot, full of soil free compost, water and stand the pot in 1-2 cm (½ -1 inch) of the right water. Pretty soon you'll have pitcher plants to give away and all the flies in your neighbourhood will live in fear.

Giant Echium

As tall as a giraffe and covered in flowers!

Grow one of these in your garden and your neighbours will think they are being invaded by aliens. A Giant Echium shoot is like a living space rocket! Up to 6 metres (20 feet) tall, half a metre (2 feet) across and covered in thousands of little blue flowers, it's a high rise party for bees! Giant Echiums come from the Canary Islands where it is hot and dry, so if you live where winters are very cold and frosty, you'll need to bring your echium indoors in its first winter, somewhere cool but frost free, like a porch or a cool windowsill.

What you need

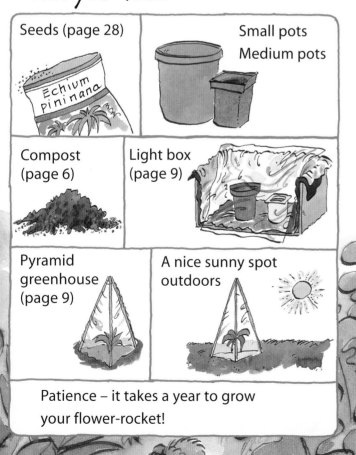

Seeds (page 28)

Echium pininana

Small pots
Medium pots

Compost (page 6)

Light box (page 9)

Pyramid greenhouse (page 9)

A nice sunny spot outdoors

Patience – it takes a year to grow your flower-rocket!

What you do

Spring Year 1

① Sow seeds thinly in small pot.

② Keep them watered and warm in the light box on a windowsill.

③ When the little plants have 3 or 4 leaves each, prick them out (see page 7) and give each plant its own medium-sized pot.

④ Keep them warm and watered, growing on a windowsill until they have six to eight leaves.

Summer Year 1

⑤ Choose a sunny spot outside, and plant each baby echium in a space of its own (or plant in a really big pot, so you can bring the plant in over winter).

⑥ Keep the plants watered and weeded and watch them spread into big rosettes of leaves. The bigger this rosette gets, the bigger your flower spike will be next year, so feed your echiums once a week to help them get huge.

Autumn and Winter Year 1

⑦ Protect plants from frost and from too much rain, with a pyramid greenhouse made of bubble wrap (or bring the pot inside).

Spring and Summer Year 2

⑧ Sow more seeds, ready for next year's echium spikes.

⑨ Watch last years plants! Your rocket spike will start to grow... and grow... and grow, and will start to flower.

More Flower Rockets

With all those flowers there should be plenty of echium seeds. When the flower spike dies, in autumn, collect the tiny dark-coloured seeds by putting a bag made of old tights over the dead flowers. When they are completely dried out, put the seeds in a paper bag and keep them dry and dark, ready for next spring.

Troubleshooting

Echium seeds are tiny and lots will germinate, so keep spare plants in case of disasters (and to give to friends). Frost and too much rain will kill echiums, so make sure they are protected in winter.

Lychee

A tropical tree from a stone

Lychee fruits have been grown in China for hundreds of years. Now they're found in lots of tropical countries and the fruits end up in supermarkets and shops all around the world. When you've peeled off the knobbly rind and eaten the white flesh, you'll find a shiny, brown stone. This is the seed of a lychee tree, and you can grow one, 2 metres (7 feet) tall, in just one summer!

Lychees like it really warm, so unless you live somewhere tropical, your lychee plant can only go outdoors on warm summer days. On cool nights and all winter it will need to stay inside.

Some fresh lychees

Medium and large pots

Compost

Somewhere really warm, like an airing cupboard

A sunny spot indoors or outside in summer

What you do

Early Spring

① Plant your lychee stone in a medium pot filled with compost. Water it well.

② Put pot inside a see-through polythene bag, and put it in a warm place – depending on where you live this might be a windowsill or an airing cupboard. It can be dark as lychees don't need light to germinate.

③ Check your seed every day. Keep it moist and as soon as the shoot pokes through the compost, put it somewhere warm and light – inside the light box on a windowsill.

④ When the roots start to show through the holes at the bottom of the pot, plant out in a BIG pot.

⑤ Your lychee tree can live outside in the summer, but needs to come in on cold, windy nights and in the winter.

Troubleshooting

Wild lychee trees live by rivers, so they like very regular watering. Always plant several lychee stones because not all the stones will sprout. Give spare plants to friends.

More Lychees

If you live where winters are cold and frosty, your lychee tree may not survive the winter, even indoors. Even if it does, it may be years before it produces fruits and seeds. So the only way to get more trees from stones, is to eat more lychees! YUM!

Where to buy Seeds and Plants

Some plants are easy to find, and others need a bit more searching out. You can get seeds of lychee, for instance, from any lychees on sale in your local supermarket or on a market stall. Voodoo Lily and Pitcher Plant are less commonly seen, and for these you might need to go to a specialist nursery.

Abyssinian Banana

Usually grown from seed, although young plants can be found in local garden centres, particularly the red-leaved Murieliae.. Seeds are often listed as Musa ensete.
UK:T&M, Chil, B&T, SBP

Cardoon

This can be listed under either vegetables or ornamentals.
UK: Chil,T&M, SBP
US: Bake, John

Giant Echium

There are many species of Echium, so it's important to specify Giant Echium, E. pinniana.
UK: Chil, B&T

Lychee

Widely obtainable as pips from fruits from the supermarket.

Pitcher Plant and Venus Fly Trap

These are getting to be more widely available. Homebase, for instance, regularly have Venus flytraps in stock.
UK: Chil, B&T, SWCP
US:What

Squirting Cucumber

UK: Chil B&T

Voodoo Lily

UK:T&M
US: Back

Walking Stick Cabbage

Sometimes listed as Walking Stick Kale or Jersey Cabbage
UK: JJ,T&M, Chil,Vic, B&T
US & Canada: Back,What, Bro

Key to Suppliers

B&T
B&T World Seeds
Paguignan, 34210 Aigues-Vives
France
http://www.b-and-t-world-seeds.com

Back
Backyardgardener LLC
PO Box 23598, Federal Way
WA 98093-0598
http://www.backyardgardener.com

Bake
Baker Creek Heirloom Seeds
2278 Baker Creek Road
Mansfield, MO 65704
1-417-924-8917
http://rareseeds.com

Bro
Brothernature
1159 Wychbury Ave
Victoria
British Columbia, BC V9A 5LI
http://www.brothernature.ca

Chil

Chiltern Seeds
Bortree Stile
Ulverston, Cumbria, LA12 7PB
01229 581137
http://www.chilternseeds.co.uk

JJ

Mrs J Johnson
Homestill
La Grande Route de St Jean
St Helier, Jersey, JE2 3FL
01534 864130
http://members.societe-jersiaise.org/philip/

John

Johnny's Selected Seeds
955 Benton Avenue
Winslow, Maine
04901
1-877-564-6697
http://www.johnnyseeds.com

SBP

Seeds by Post
Woodlands Farm
Trinity Road
Freasley, Tamworth
Staffs, B78 2EY
01827 251511
http://www.seedsbypost.co.uk

SWCP

South West Carnivorous Plants
Blackwater Nursery
Blackwater Road
Culmstock, Devon, EX15 3HG
01823 681669
http://www.littleshopofhorrors.co.uk

Seed

Jim Johnson, Seedman
3421 Bream St.
Gautier, MS 39553
http://www.seedman.com

T&M

Thompson & Morgan (UK) Ltd.
Poplar Lane
Ipswich, Suffolk, IP8 3BU
0844 248 5383
http://www.thompson-morgan.com

Vic

Victoriana Nursery Gardens
Challock
nr Ashford, Kent, TN25 4DG
01233 740529
http://www.victoriananursery.co.uk

What

Whatcom Seed Company
PO Box 40700
Eugene, Oregon 97404
1-866-475-1179
http://seedrack.com

Glossary

Habitat - is where a plant or animal lives and grows best.

De-ionised water - is extra pure water that's used in car batteries or in steam irons. You can buy it in shops and it's a good replacement for rain water for watering insectivorous plants like the Venus Fly Trap and Pitcher Plant.

Pollination - is when pollen – from the stamens, which are the male parts of the flower – gets onto the stigma which is the female part.
and
Fertilisation - is what happens next! Pollen grains travel down the stigma and join with the ova, to make a seed.

Sowing - is the proper word for planting seeds. You sow seeds, and plant plants!

Germination - is when seeds sprout and start to grow

Planting out - is when you take young plants out of their pots and plant them outside, to give them more space to grow.

Pricking out - is when tiny baby plants are moved to bigger pots to give them more space

Transplanting - is when you dig a plant up, or take it from its pot, and plant it somewhere else.

Spathe - is the name for the deep red petal of the voodoo lily. It isn't really a petal at all but a kind of leaf.

Corm - is a fat underground stem, where a plant stores food. A corm can survive when the rest of the plant has died and shrivelled up, to grow again when conditions are better.

For Janice and Colin

JANETTA OTTER-BARRY BOOKS

First published in Great Britain in 2010 and in the USA in 2011 by Frances Lincoln Children's Books, 4 Torriano Mews, Torriano Avenue, London NW5 2RZ
www.franceslincoln.com

Grow Your Own Monsters copyright © Frances Lincoln Limited 2010
Text copyright © Nicola Davies and Simon Hickmott 2010
Illustrations copyright © Scoular Anderson 2010
Photographs:
cover, endpapers, pages 16, 20, 22 and 24 copyright © Clive Boursnell
page 10 © Emy Smith, page 12 © Robert Down, page 14 © Rosemary Kautzky –
all photographersdirect.com
page 18 © Philip Johnson

All rights reserved

A catalogue record for this book is available from the British Library.

ISBN 978-1-84507-833-1

Printed in Dongguan, Guangdong, China by Toppan Leefung in May 2010

9 8 7 6 5 4 3 2 1